A YEAR OF
QUOTES FROM
**CLASSIC
LITERATURE**

" TIME LINES **2024** "

**17-MONTH
PLANNER**

U

**UNION
SQUARE
& CO.**

NEW YORK

2023

JANUARY 2023

S	M	T	W	T	F	S
1	2	3	4	5	6	7
8	9	10	11	12	13	14
15	16	17	18	19	20	21
22	23	24	25	26	27	28
29	30	31				

FEBRUARY 2023

S	M	T	W	T	F	S
			1	2	3	4
5	6	7	8	9	10	11
12	13	14	15	16	17	18
19	20	21	22	23	24	25
26	27	28				

MARCH 2023

S	M	T	W	T	F	S
			1	2	3	4
5	6	7	8	9	10	11
12	13	14	15	16	17	18
19	20	21	22	23	24	25
26	27	28	29	30	31	

APRIL 2023

S	M	T	W	T	F	S
						1
2	3	4	5	6	7	8
9	10	11	12	13	14	15
16	17	18	19	20	21	22
23	24	25	26	27	28	29
30						

MAY 2023

S	M	T	W	T	F	S
	1	2	3	4	5	6
7	8	9	10	11	12	13
14	15	16	17	18	19	20
21	22	23	24	25	26	27
28	29	30	31			

JUNE 2023

S	M	T	W	T	F	S
				1	2	3
4	5	6	7	8	9	10
11	12	13	14	15	16	17
18	19	20	21	22	23	24
25	26	27	28	29	30	

JULY 2023

S	M	T	W	T	F	S
						1
2	3	4	5	6	7	8
9	10	11	12	13	14	15
16	17	18	19	20	21	22
23	24	25	26	27	28	29
30	31					

AUGUST 2023

S	M	T	W	T	F	S
		1	2	3	4	5
6	7	8	9	10	11	12
13	14	15	16	17	18	19
20	21	22	23	24	25	26
27	28	29	30	31		

SEPTEMBER 2023

S	M	T	W	T	F	S
					1	2
3	4	5	6	7	8	9
10	11	12	13	14	15	16
17	18	19	20	21	22	23
24	25	26	27	28	29	30

OCTOBER 2023

S	M	T	W	T	F	S
1	2	3	4	5	6	7
8	9	10	11	12	13	14
15	16	17	18	19	20	21
22	23	24	25	26	27	28
29	30	31				

NOVEMBER 2023

S	M	T	W	T	F	S
			1	2	3	4
5	6	7	8	9	10	11
12	13	14	15	16	17	18
19	20	21	22	23	24	25
26	27	28	29	30		

DECEMBER 2023

S	M	T	W	T	F	S
					1	2
3	4	5	6	7	8	9
10	11	12	13	14	15	16
17	18	19	20	21	22	23
24	25	26	27	28	29	30
31						

2024

JANUARY 2024

S	M	T	W	T	F	S
	1	2	3	4	5	6
7	8	9	10	11	12	13
14	15	16	17	18	19	20
21	22	23	24	25	26	27
28	29	30	31			

FEBRUARY 2024

S	M	T	W	T	F	S
				1	2	3
4	5	6	7	8	9	10
11	12	13	14	15	16	17
18	19	20	21	22	23	24
25	26	27	28	29		

MARCH 2024

S	M	T	W	T	F	S
					1	2
3	4	5	6	7	8	9
10	11	12	13	14	15	16
17	18	19	20	21	22	23
24	25	26	27	28	29	30
31						

APRIL 2024

S	M	T	W	T	F	S
	1	2	3	4	5	6
7	8	9	10	11	12	13
14	15	16	17	18	19	20
21	22	23	24	25	26	27
28	29	30				

MAY 2024

S	M	T	W	T	F	S
			1	2	3	4
5	6	7	8	9	10	11
12	13	14	15	16	17	18
19	20	21	22	23	24	25
26	27	28	29	30	31	

JUNE 2024

S	M	T	W	T	F	S
						1
2	3	4	5	6	7	8
9	10	11	12	13	14	15
16	17	18	19	20	21	22
23	24	25	26	27	28	29
30						

JULY 2024

S	M	T	W	T	F	S
	1	2	3	4	5	6
7	8	9	10	11	12	13
14	15	16	17	18	19	20
21	22	23	24	25	26	27
28	29	30	31			

AUGUST 2024

S	M	T	W	T	F	S
				1	2	3
4	5	6	7	8	9	10
11	12	13	14	15	16	17
18	19	20	21	22	23	24
25	26	27	28	29	30	31

SEPTEMBER 2024

S	M	T	W	T	F	S
1	2	3	4	5	6	7
8	9	10	11	12	13	14
15	16	17	18	19	20	21
22	23	24	25	26	27	28
29	30					

OCTOBER 2024

S	M	T	W	T	F	S
		1	2	3	4	5
6	7	8	9	10	11	12
13	14	15	16	17	18	19
20	21	22	23	24	25	26
27	28	29	30	31		

NOVEMBER 2024

S	M	T	W	T	F	S
					1	2
3	4	5	6	7	8	9
10	11	12	13	14	15	16
17	18	19	20	21	22	23
24	25	26	27	28	29	30

DECEMBER 2024

S	M	T	W	T	F	S
1	2	3	4	5	6	7
8	9	10	11	12	13	14
15	16	17	18	19	20	21
22	23	24	25	26	27	28
29	30	31				

"It was a never to be forgotten summer . . . one of those summers which, in a fortunate combination of delightful weather, delightful friends and delightful doing, come as near to perfection as anything can come in this world."

—L. M. Montgomery, *Anne's House of Dreams* (1917)

notes for august

AUGUST

2023

SUN	MON	TUE
		1 Full Moon ○
6	7	8 Last Quarter Moon ◑
13	14	15
20	21	22
27	28 Summer Bank Holiday (UK)	29

WED	THU	FRI	SAT
2	3	4	5
9	10	11	12
16 New Moon ●	17	18	19
23	24 First Quarter Moon ◖	25	26
30 Full Moon ○	31		

31 MONDAY

---

1 TUESDAY

Full Moon ○

---

2 WEDNESDAY

---

3 THURSDAY

4 FRIDAY

---

5 SATURDAY

6 SUNDAY

NOTES

- Primo Levi, b. 7/31/1919
- Herman Melville, b. 8/1/1819
- James Baldwin, b. 8/2/1924
- Isabel Allende, b. 8/2/1942
- P. D. James, b. 8/3/1920
- Percy Bysshe Shelley, b. 8/4/1792

AUGUST 2023

S	M	T	W	T	F	S
		1	2	3	4	5
6	7	8	9	10	11	12
13	14	15	16	17	18	19
20	21	22	23	24	25	26
27	28	29	30	31		

SEPTEMBER 2023

S	M	T	W	T	F	S
					1	2
3	4	5	6	7	8	9
10	11	12	13	14	15	16
17	18	19	20	21	22	23
24	25	26	27	28	29	30

7 MONDAY

8 TUESDAY

Last Quarter Moon ☽

9 WEDNESDAY

10 THURSDAY

11 FRIDAY

12 SATURDAY

13 SUNDAY

NOTES

- Guy de Maupassant, b. 8/5/1850
- Sara Teasdale, b. 8/8/1884
- Daniel Keyes, b. 8/9/1927
- Jorge Amado, b. 8/10/1912
- Suzanne Collins, b. 8/10/1962
- Alex Haley, b. 8/11/1921
- William Goldman, b. 8/12/1931

AUGUST 2023						
S	M	T	W	T	F	S
		1	2	3	4	5
6	7	8	9	10	11	12
13	14	15	16	17	18	19
20	21	22	23	24	25	26
27	28	29	30	31		

SEPTEMBER 2023						
S	M	T	W	T	F	S
					1	2
3	4	5	6	7	8	9
10	11	12	13	14	15	16
17	18	19	20	21	22	23
24	25	26	27	28	29	30

14 MONDAY

15 TUESDAY

16 WEDNESDAY

New Moon ●

17 THURSDAY

18 FRIDAY

---

19 SATURDAY

20 SUNDAY

- Letitia Elizabeth Landon, b. 8/14/1802
- Edna Ferber, b. 8/15/1885
- Charles Bukowski, 8/16/1920
- V. S. Naipaul, b. 8/17/1932
- Ogden Nash, b. 8/19/1902
- Frank McCourt, b. 8/19/1930
- H. P. Lovecraft, 8/20/1890

AUGUST 2023

S	M	T	W	T	F	S
		1	2	3	4	5
6	7	8	9	10	11	12
13	14	15	16	17	18	19
20	21	22	23	24	25	26
27	28	29	30	31		

SEPTEMBER 2023

S	M	T	W	T	F	S
					1	2
3	4	5	6	7	8	9
10	11	12	13	14	15	16
17	18	19	20	21	22	23
24	25	26	27	28	29	30

21 MONDAY

22 TUESDAY

23 WEDNESDAY

24 THURSDAY

First Quarter Moon ◐

25 FRIDAY

26 SATURDAY

27 SUNDAY

- Ray Bradbury, b. 8/22/1920
- Annie Proulx, b. 8/22/1935
- Dorothy Parker, b. 8/22/1893
- Jorge Luis Borges, b. 8/24/1899
- A. S. Byatt b. 8/24/1936
- Martin Amis, b. 8/25/1949
- Theodore Dreiser, b. 8/27/1871

AUGUST 2023

S	M	T	W	T	F	S
		1	2	3	4	5
6	7	8	9	10	11	12
13	14	15	16	17	18	19
20	21	22	23	24	25	26
27	28	29	30	31		

SEPTEMBER 2023

S	M	T	W	T	F	S
					1	2
3	4	5	6	7	8	9
10	11	12	13	14	15	16
17	18	19	20	21	22	23
24	25	26	27	28	29	30

28 MONDAY

Summer Bank Holiday (UK)

29 TUESDAY

30 WEDNESDAY

Full Moon ○

31 THURSDAY

1 FRIDAY

2 SATURDAY

3 SUNDAY

NOTES

- Johann Wolfgang von Goethe, b. 8/28/1749
- Rita Dove, b. 8/28/1952
- Oliver Wendell Holmes Sr., b. 8/29/1809
- Mary Shelley, b. 8/30/1797
- Edgar Rice Burroughs, b. 9/1/1875

AUGUST 2023						
S	M	T	W	T	F	S
		1	2	3	4	5
6	7	8	9	10	11	12
13	14	15	16	17	18	19
20	21	22	23	24	25	26
27	28	29	30	31		

SEPTEMBER 2023						
S	M	T	W	T	F	S
					1	2
3	4	5	6	7	8	9
10	11	12	13	14	15	16
17	18	19	20	21	22	23
24	25	26	27	28	29	30

SEP
TEM
BER

SEPTEMBER

Sep

BER
TEM
S

"When we paddled on the river through that fine-grained September air, did there not appear to be something new going on under the sparkling surface of the stream, a shaking of props, at least, so that we made haste in order to be up in time?"

—Henry David Thoreau, "Autumnal Tints," *Atlantic Monthly* (October 1862)

notes for september

SEPTEMBER

2024

SUN	MON	TUE
3	4 Labor Day (US, CAN)	5
10	11	12
17	18	19
24 Yom Kippur (begins at sundown)	25	26

WED	THU	FRI	SAT
		1	2
6 Last Quarter Moon ◑	7	8	9
13	14 New Moon ●	15 Rosh Hashanah (begins at sundown)	16
20	21	22 First Quarter Moon ◐	23
27	28	29 Full Moon ○	30

SEPTEMBER 2023

4 MONDAY

Labor Day (US, CAN)

5 TUESDAY

6 WEDNESDAY

Last Quarter Moon ◗

7 THURSDAY

8 FRIDAY

9 SATURDAY

10 SUNDAY

NOTES

- Richard Wright, b. 9/4/1908
- Robert M. Pirsig, 9/6/1928
- Jennifer Egan, b. 9/7/1962
- Siegfried Sassoon, b. 9/8/1886
- Ann Beattie, b. 9/8/1947
- Leo Tolstoy, b. 9/9/1828
- Jared Diamond, b. 9/10/1937

SEPTEMBER 2023

S	M	T	W	T	F	S
					1	2
3	4	5	6	7	8	9
10	11	12	13	14	15	16
17	18	19	20	21	22	23
24	25	26	27	28	29	30

OCTOBER 2023

S	M	T	W	T	F	S
1	2	3	4	5	6	7
8	9	10	11	12	13	14
15	16	17	18	19	20	21
22	23	24	25	26	27	28
29	30	31				

11 MONDAY

12 TUESDAY

13 WEDNESDAY

14 THURSDAY

New Moon ●

15 FRIDAY

Rosh Hashanah (begins at sundown)

16 SATURDAY

17 SUNDAY

NOTES

- O. Henry, b. 9/11/1862
- D. H. Lawrence, b. 9/11/1885
- Michael Ondaatje, b. 9/12/1943
- Roald Dahl, b. 9/13/1916
- James Fenimore Cooper, b. 9/15/1789
- Agatha Christie, b. 9/15/1890
- Ken Kesey, b. 9/17/1935

SEPTEMBER 2023

S	M	T	W	T	F	S
					1	2
3	4	5	6	7	8	9
10	11	12	13	14	15	16
17	18	19	20	21	22	23
24	25	26	27	28	29	30

OCTOBER 2023

S	M	T	W	T	F	S
1	2	3	4	5	6	7
8	9	10	11	12	13	14
15	16	17	18	19	20	21
22	23	24	25	26	27	28
29	30	31				

18 MONDAY

19 TUESDAY

20 WEDNESDAY

21 THURSDAY

22 FRIDAY

First Quarter Moon ◐

23 SATURDAY

24 SUNDAY

Yom Kippur (begins at sundown)

NOTES

- Samuel Johnson, b. 9/18/1709
- William Golding, b. 9/19/1911
- Upton Sinclair, b. 9/20/1878
- George R. R. Martin, b. 9/20/1948
- H. G. Wells, 9/21/1866
- Stephen King, b. 9/21/1947
- Rosamunde Pilcher, b. 9/22/1924
- F. Scott Fitzgerald, b. 9/24/1896

SEPTEMBER 2023						
S	M	T	W	T	F	S
					1	2
3	4	5	6	7	8	9
10	11	12	13	14	15	16
17	18	19	20	21	22	23
24	25	26	27	28	29	30

OCTOBER 2023						
S	M	T	W	T	F	S
1	2	3	4	5	6	7
8	9	10	11	12	13	14
15	16	17	18	19	20	21
22	23	24	25	26	27	28
29	30	31				

25 MONDAY

26 TUESDAY

27 WEDNESDAY

28 THURSDAY

29 FRIDAY

Full Moon ○

30 SATURDAY

1 SUNDAY

NOTES

- William Faulkner, b. 9/25/1897
- bell hooks, b. 9/25/1952
- T. S. Eliot, b. 9/26/1888
- Miguel de Cervantes, b. 9/29/1547
- Truman Capote, b. 9/30/1924
- Elie Wiesel, b. 9/30/1928
- Laura Esquivel, b. 9/30/1950
- Ta-Nehisi Coates, b. 9/30/1975

SEPTEMBER 2023						
S	M	T	W	T	F	S
					1	2
3	4	5	6	7	8	9
10	11	12	13	14	15	16
17	18	19	20	21	22	23
24	25	26	27	28	29	30

OCTOBER 2023						
S	M	T	W	T	F	S
1	2	3	4	5	6	7
8	9	10	11	12	13	14
15	16	17	18	19	20	21
22	23	24	25	26	27	28
29	30	31				

OC
TO
BER

OCTOB

"October is the treasurer of the year,
   And all the months pay bounty to her store;
The fields and orchards still their tribute bear,
   And fill her brimming coffers more and more."

—Paul Laurence Dunbar, "October" (c. 1900)

notes for october

OCTOBER

2024

SUN	MON	TUE
1	2	3
8	9 Indigenous Peoples' Day Columbus Day (US) Thanksgiving (CAN)	10
15	16	17
22	23	24
29	30	31 Halloween

WED	THU	FRI	SAT
4	5	6 Last Quarter Moon ◑	7
11	12	13	14 New Moon ●
18	19	20	21 First Quarter Moon ◐
25	26	27	28 Full Moon ○

2 MONDAY

---

3 TUESDAY

---

4 WEDNESDAY

---

5 THURSDAY

6 FRIDAY

Last Quarter Moon ◑

7 SATURDAY

8 SUNDAY

NOTES

- Graham Greene, b. 10/2/1904
- Gore Vidal, b. 10/3/1925
- Jackie Collins, b. 10/4/1937
- Anne Rice, b. 10/4/1941
- Václav Havel, b. 10/5/1936
- Thomas Keneally, b. 10/7/1935
- Frank Herbert, b. 10/8/1920

OCTOBER 2023

S	M	T	W	T	F	S
1	2	3	4	5	6	7
8	9	10	11	12	13	14
15	16	17	18	19	20	21
22	23	24	25	26	27	28
29	30	31				

NOVEMBER 2023

S	M	T	W	T	F	S
			1	2	3	4
5	6	7	8	9	10	11
12	13	14	15	16	17	18
19	20	21	22	23	24	25
26	27	28	29	30		

9 MONDAY

Indigenous Peoples' Day
Columbus Day (US)
Thanksgiving (CAN)

10 TUESDAY

11 WEDNESDAY

12 THURSDAY

13 FRIDAY

14 SATURDAY

15 SUNDAY

New Moon ●

NOTES

- James Clavell, b. 10/10/1921
- Elmore Leonard, b. 10/11/1925
- Richard Price, b. 10/12/1949
- e. e. cummings, b. 10/14/1894
- P. G. Wodehouse, b. 10/15/1881
- Ntozake Shange, b. 10/18/1948

OCTOBER 2023

S	M	T	W	T	F	S
1	2	3	4	5	6	7
8	9	10	11	12	13	14
15	16	17	18	19	20	21
22	23	24	25	26	27	28
29	30	31				

NOVEMBER 2023

S	M	T	W	T	F	S
			1	2	3	4
5	6	7	8	9	10	11
12	13	14	15	16	17	18
19	20	21	22	23	24	25
26	27	28	29	30		

OCTOBER 2023

16 MONDAY

17 TUESDAY

18 WEDNESDAY

19 THURSDAY

20 FRIDAY

21 SATURDAY

22 SUNDAY

First Quarter Moon ◑

NOTES

- Oscar Wilde, b. 10/16/1854
- Günter Grass, b. 10/16/1927
- Arthur Miller b. 10/17/1915
- Terry McMillan, b. 10/18/1951
- John le Carré, b. 10/19/1931
- Samuel Taylor Coleridge, b. 10/21/1772
- Ursula K. Le Guin, b. 10/21/1929
- Doris Lessing, b. 10/22/1919

OCTOBER 2023

S	M	T	W	T	F	S
1	2	3	4	5	6	7
8	9	10	11	12	13	14
15	16	17	18	19	20	21
22	23	24	25	26	27	28
29	30	31				

NOVEMBER 2023

S	M	T	W	T	F	S
			1	2	3	4
5	6	7	8	9	10	11
12	13	14	15	16	17	18
19	20	21	22	23	24	25
26	27	28	29	30		

OCTOBER 2023

23 MONDAY

24 TUESDAY

25 WEDNESDAY

26 THURSDAY

27 FRIDAY

---

28 SATURDAY

29 SUNDAY

Full Moon ○

- Michael Crichton, b. 10/23/1942
- Denise Levertov, b. 10/24/1923
- Anne Tyler, b. 10/25/1941
- Zadie Smith, b. 10/25/1975
- Dylan Thomas, b. 10/27/1914
- Sylvia Plath, b. 10/27/1932

OCTOBER 2023

S	M	T	W	T	F	S
1	2	3	4	5	6	7
8	9	10	11	12	13	14
15	16	17	18	19	20	21
22	23	24	25	26	27	28
29	30	31				

NOVEMBER 2023

S	M	T	W	T	F	S
			1	2	3	4
5	6	7	8	9	10	11
12	13	14	15	16	17	18
19	20	21	22	23	24	25
26	27	28	29	30		

30 MONDAY

31 TUESDAY

Halloween

1 WEDNESDAY

2 THURSDAY

3 FRIDAY

4 SATURDAY

5 SUNDAY

Daylight Saving Time Ends (US, CAN)
Last Quarter Moon ◑

NOTES

- Robert Caro, b. 10/30/1935
- John Keats, b. 10/31/1795
- Stephen Crane, b. 11/1/1871
- Susanna Clarke, b. 11/1/1959
- William Cullen Bryant, b. 11/3/1794
- Ida Tarbell, b. 11/5/1857

OCTOBER 2023

S	M	T	W	T	F	S
1	2	3	4	5	6	7
8	9	10	11	12	13	14
15	16	17	18	19	20	21
22	23	24	25	26	27	28
29	30	31				

NOVEMBER 2023

S	M	T	W	T	F	S
			1	2	3	4
5	6	7	8	9	10	11
12	13	14	15	16	17	18
19	20	21	22	23	24	25
26	27	28	29	30		

NOVEMBER

NOVEMBER

NO
VEM
BER

novembe

> "It is also November. The noons are more laconic and the sunsets sterner, and Gibraltar lights make the village foreign. November always seemed to me the Norway of the year."
>
> —Emily Dickinson, in a letter to her friend Elizabeth Holland (November 1865)

notes for november

NOVEMBER

2024

SUN	MON	TUE
5 Daylight Saving Time Ends (US, CAN) Last Quarter Moon ◗	**6**	**7** Election Day (US)
12	**13** New Moon ●	**14**
19	**20** First Quarter Moon ◑	**21**
26	**27** Full Moon ○	**28**

WED	THU	FRI	SAT
1	2	3	4
8	9	10	11 Veterans Day (US)
15	16	17	18
22	23 Thanksgiving (US)	24	25
29	30		

6 MONDAY

7 TUESDAY

Election Day (US)

8 WEDNESDAY

9 THURSDAY

10 FRIDAY

---

11 SATURDAY

12 SUNDAY

Veterans Day (US)

NOTES

- Colson Whitehead, b. 11/6/1969
- Albert Camus, b. 11/7/1913
- Bram Stoker, b. 11/8/1847
- Margaret Mitchell, b. 11/8/1900
- Kazuo Ishiguro, b. 11/8/1954
- Neil Gaiman, b. 11/10/1960
- Fyodor Dostoevsky, b. 11/11/1821
- Carlos Fuentes, b. 11/11/1928
- Kurt Vonnegut, b. 11/11/1922

\	\	\	NOVEMBER 2023	\	\	\
S	M	T	W	T	F	S
			1	2	3	4
5	6	7	8	9	10	11
12	13	14	15	16	17	18
19	20	21	22	23	24	25
26	27	28	29	30		

\	\	\	DECEMBER 2023	\	\	\
S	M	T	W	T	F	S
					1	2
3	4	5	6	7	8	9
10	11	12	13	14	15	16
17	18	19	20	21	22	23
24	25	26	27	28	29	30
31						

13 MONDAY

New Moon ●

14 TUESDAY

15 WEDNESDAY

16 THURSDAY

17 FRIDAY

18 SATURDAY

19 SUNDAY

- Robert Louis Stevenson, b. 11/13/1850
- Astrid Lindgren, b. 11/14/1907
- J. G. Ballard, b. 11/15/1930
- Liane Moriarty, b. 11/15/1966
- Chinua Achebe, b. 11/16/1930
- Margaret Atwood, b. 11/18/1939

NOVEMBER 2023

S	M	T	W	T	F	S
			1	2	3	4
5	6	7	8	9	10	11
12	13	14	15	16	17	18
19	20	21	22	23	24	25
26	27	28	29	30		

DECEMBER 2023

S	M	T	W	T	F	S
					1	2
3	4	5	6	7	8	9
10	11	12	13	14	15	16
17	18	19	20	21	22	23
24	25	26	27	28	29	30
31						

20 MONDAY

First Quarter Moon ☽

21 TUESDAY

22 WEDNESDAY

23 THURSDAY

Thanksgiving (US)

24 FRIDAY

25 SATURDAY

26 SUNDAY

NOTES

- Nadine Gordimer, b. 11/20/1923
- Don DeLillo, b. 11/20/1936
- Isaac Bashevis Singer, b. 11/21/1902
- George Eliot, b. 11/22/1819
- André Gide, b. 11/22/1869
- Frances Hodgson Burnett,
  b. 11/24/1849
- Arundhati Roy, b. 11/24/1961
- Eugène Ionesco, b. 11/26/1909

NOVEMBER 2023

S	M	T	W	T	F	S
			1	2	3	4
5	6	7	8	9	10	11
12	13	14	15	16	17	18
19	20	21	22	23	24	25
26	27	28	29	30		

DECEMBER 2023

S	M	T	W	T	F	S
					1	2
3	4	5	6	7	8	9
10	11	12	13	14	15	16
17	18	19	20	21	22	23
24	25	26	27	28	29	30
31						

27 MONDAY

Full Moon ○

28 TUESDAY

29 WEDNESDAY

30 THURSDAY

1 FRIDAY

2 SATURDAY

3 SUNDAY

NOTES

- James Agee, b. 11/27/1909
- Louisa May Alcott, b. 11/29/1832
- C. S. Lewis, b. 11/29/1898
- Madeleine L'Engle, b. 11/29/1918
- Mark Twain, b. 11/30/1835
- L. M. Montgomery, b. 11/30/1874
- Candace Bushnell, b. 12/1/1958
- T. C. Boyle, b. 12/2/1948
- Ann Patchett, b. 12/2/1963

NOVEMBER 2023

S	M	T	W	T	F	S
			1	2	3	4
5	6	7	8	9	10	11
12	13	14	15	16	17	18
19	20	21	22	23	24	25
26	27	28	29	30		

DECEMBER 2023

S	M	T	W	T	F	S
					1	2
3	4	5	6	7	8	9
10	11	12	13	14	15	16
17	18	19	20	21	22	23
24	25	26	27	28	29	30
31						

DECEMBER

december

DECEMBER

DECEMBER

"On cold December fragrant chaplets blow,
And heavy harvests nod beneath the snow."

—Alexander Pope, *The Dunciad* (1728)

notes for december

DECEMBER

2024

SUN	MON	TUE
3	4	5 Last Quarter Moon ◐
10	11	12 New Moon ●
17	18	19 First Quarter Moon ◑
24 New Year's Eve **31**	25 Christmas Day	26 Kwanzaa Boxing Day (CAN, UK) Full Moon ○

WED	THU	FRI	SAT
		1	2
6	7 **Hanukkah** **(begins at sunset)**	8	9
13	14	15	16
20	21	22	23
27	28	29	30

DECEMBER 2023

4 MONDAY

---

5 TUESDAY

Last Quarter Moon ◗

---

6 WEDNESDAY

---

7 THURSDAY

Hanukkah (begins at sundown)

8 FRIDAY

9 SATURDAY

10 SUNDAY

NOTES

- Rainier Maria Rilke, b. 12/4/1875
- Joan Didion, b. 12/5/1934
- Calvin Trillin, b. 12/5/1935
- Willa Cather, b. 12/7/1873
- James Thurber, b. 12/8/1894
- John Milton, b. 12/9/1608
- Emily Dickinson, b. 12/10/1830

DECEMBER 2023

S	M	T	W	T	F	S
					1	2
3	4	5	6	7	8	9
10	11	12	13	14	15	16
17	18	19	20	21	22	23
24	25	26	27	28	29	30
31						

JANUARY 2024

S	M	T	W	T	F	S
	1	2	3	4	5	6
7	8	9	10	11	12	13
14	15	16	17	18	19	20
21	22	23	24	25	26	27
28	29	30	31			

DECEMBER 2023

11 MONDAY

12 TUESDAY

New Moon ●

13 WEDNESDAY

14 THURSDAY

15 FRIDAY

16 SATURDAY

17 SUNDAY

NOTES

- Naguib Mahfouz, b. 12/11/1911
- Aleksandr Solzhenitsyn, b. 12/11/1918
- Colleen Hoover, b. 12/11/1979
- Gustave Flaubert, b. 12/12/1821
- Shirley Jackson, b. 12/14/1916
- Edna O'Brien, b. 12/15/1930
- Jane Austen, b. 12/16/1775

DECEMBER 2023

S	M	T	W	T	F	S
					1	2
3	4	5	6	7	8	9
10	11	12	13	14	15	16
17	18	19	20	21	22	23
24	25	26	27	28	29	30
31						

JANUARY 2024

S	M	T	W	T	F	S
	1	2	3	4	5	6
7	8	9	10	11	12	13
14	15	16	17	18	19	20
21	22	23	24	25	26	27
28	29	30	31			

18 MONDAY

19 TUESDAY

First Quarter Moon ◑

20 WEDNESDAY

21 THURSDAY

22 FRIDAY

23 SATURDAY

24 SUNDAY

NOTES

- H. H. Munro (Saki), b. 12/18/1870
- Kate Atkinson, b. 12/20/1951
- Sandra Cisneros, b. 12/20/1954
- Rebecca West, b. 12/21/1892
- Donna Tartt, b. 12/23/1963
- Mary Higgins Clark, b. 12/24/1927

DECEMBER 2023

S	M	T	W	T	F	S
					1	2
3	4	5	6	7	8	9
10	11	12	13	14	15	16
17	18	19	20	21	22	23
24	25	26	27	28	29	30
31						

JANUARY 2024

S	M	T	W	T	F	S
	1	2	3	4	5	6
7	8	9	10	11	12	13
14	15	16	17	18	19	20
21	22	23	24	25	26	27
28	29	30	31			

DECEMBER 2023

25 MONDAY

Christmas Day

26 TUESDAY

Kwanzaa
Boxing Day (CAN, UK)
Full Moon ○

27 WEDNESDAY

28 THURSDAY

29 FRIDAY

30 SATURDAY

31 SUNDAY

New Year's Eve

NOTES

- Carlos Castañeda, b. 12/25/1925
- Henry Miller, b. 12/26/1891
- David Sedaris, b. 12/26/1956
- Stan Lee, b. 12/28/1922
- William Gaddis, b. 12/29/1922
- Paul Bowles, b. 12/30/1910
- Junot Díaz, b. 12/31/1968

DECEMBER 2023						
S	M	T	W	T	F	S
					1	2
3	4	5	6	7	8	9
10	11	12	13	14	15	16
17	18	19	20	21	22	23
24	25	26	27	28	29	30
31						

JANUARY 2024						
S	M	T	W	T	F	S
	1	2	3	4	5	6
7	8	9	10	11	12	13
14	15	16	17	18	19	20
21	22	23	24	25	26	27
28	29	30	31			

JANUARY

**"Cheer up! Don't give way.
A new heart for a New Year, always!"**

—Charles Dickens, *The Chimes* (1844)

notes for january

JANUARY

2024

SUN	MON	TUE
	1 New Year's Day	**2**
7	**8**	**9**
14	**15** Martin Luther King Jr. Day	**16**
21	**22**	**23**
28	**29**	**30**

WED	THU	FRI	SAT
3 Last Quarter Moon ◑	**4**	**5**	**6**
10	**11** New Moon ●	**12**	**13**
17 First Quarter Moon ◐	**18**	**19**	**20**
24	**25** Full Moon ○	**26** Australia Day	**27**
31			

JANUARY 2024

1 MONDAY

New Year's Day

2 TUESDAY

3 WEDNESDAY

Last Quarter Moon ◑

4 THURSDAY

5 FRIDAY

6 SATURDAY

7 SUNDAY

NOTES

- E. M. Forster, b. 1/1/1879
- J. D. Salinger, b. 1/1/1919
- Isaac Asimov, b. c. 1/2/1920
- J. R. R. Tolkien, b. 1/3/1892
- Erik Larson, b. 1/3/1954
- Umberto Eco, b. 1/5/1932
- E. L. Doctorow, b. 1/6/1931
- Carl Sandburg, b. 1/6/1878
- Zora Neale Hurston, b. 1/7/1891

JANUARY 2024

S	M	T	W	T	F	S
	1	2	3	4	5	6
7	8	9	10	11	12	13
14	15	16	17	18	19	20
21	22	23	24	25	26	27
28	29	30	31			

FEBRUARY 2024

S	M	T	W	T	F	S
				1	2	3
4	5	6	7	8	9	10
11	12	13	14	15	16	17
18	19	20	21	22	23	24
25	26	27	28	29		

8 MONDAY

9 TUESDAY

10 WEDNESDAY

11 THURSDAY

New Moon ●

12 FRIDAY

---

13 SATURDAY

14 SUNDAY

NOTES

- Wilkie Collins, b. 1/8/1824
- Simone de Beauvoir, b. 1/9/1908
- Diana Gabaldon, b. 1/11/1952
- Jack London, b. 1/12/1876
- Haruki Murakami, b. 1/12/1949
- Jay McInerney, b. 1/13/1955
- Yukio Mishima, b. 1/14/1925

JANUARY 2024						
S	M	T	W	T	F	S
	1	2	3	4	5	6
7	8	9	10	11	12	13
14	15	16	17	18	19	20
21	22	23	24	25	26	27
28	29	30	31			

FEBRUARY 2024						
S	M	T	W	T	F	S
				1	2	3
4	5	6	7	8	9	10
11	12	13	14	15	16	17
18	19	20	21	22	23	24
25	26	27	28	29		

15 MONDAY

Martin Luther King Jr. Day

16 TUESDAY

17 WEDNESDAY

First Quarter Moon ◑

18 THURSDAY

19 FRIDAY

20 SATURDAY

21 SUNDAY

NOTES

- Susan Sontag, b. 1/16/1933
- Anne Brontë, b. 1/17/1820
- A. A. Milne, b. 1/18/1882
- Edgar Allan Poe, b. 1/19/1809
- Patricia Highsmith, b. 1/19/1921

JANUARY 2024						
S	M	T	W	T	F	S
	1	2	3	4	5	6
7	8	9	10	11	12	13
14	15	16	17	18	19	20
21	22	23	24	25	26	27
28	29	30	31			

FEBRUARY 2024						
S	M	T	W	T	F	S
				1	2	3
4	5	6	7	8	9	10
11	12	13	14	15	16	17
18	19	20	21	22	23	24
25	26	27	28	29		

JANUARY 2024

22 MONDAY

23 TUESDAY

24 WEDNESDAY

25 THURSDAY

Full Moon ○

26 FRIDAY

Australia Day

---

27 SATURDAY

28 SUNDAY

NOTES

- Edith Wharton, b. 1/24/1862
- Virginia Woolf, b. 1/25/1882
- Angela Davis, b. 1/26/1944
- Lewis Carroll, b. 1/27/1832
- Colette, b. 1/28/1873

JANUARY 2024

S	M	T	W	T	F	S
	1	2	3	4	5	6
7	8	9	10	11	12	13
14	15	16	17	18	19	20
21	22	23	24	25	26	27
28	29	30	31			

FEBRUARY 2024

S	M	T	W	T	F	S
				1	2	3
4	5	6	7	8	9	10
11	12	13	14	15	16	17
18	19	20	21	22	23	24
25	26	27	28	29		

29 MONDAY

30 TUESDAY

31 WEDNESDAY

1 THURSDAY

2 FRIDAY

Groundhog Day
Last Quarter Moon ◗

3 SATURDAY

4 SUNDAY

NOTES

- Anton Chekhov, b. 1/29/1860
- Zane Grey, b. 1/31/1872
- John O'Hara, b. 1/31/1905
- Norman Mailer, b. 1/31/1923
- Langston Hughes, b. 2/1/1901
- James Joyce, b. 2/2/1882
- Ayn Rand, b. 2/2/1905
- Gertrude Stein, b. 2/3/1874

JANUARY 2024

S	M	T	W	T	F	S
	1	2	3	4	5	6
7	8	9	10	11	12	13
14	15	16	17	18	19	20
21	22	23	24	25	26	27
28	29	30	31			

FEBRUARY 2024

S	M	T	W	T	F	S
				1	2	3
4	5	6	7	8	9	10
11	12	13	14	15	16	17
18	19	20	21	22	23	24
25	26	27	28	29		

FEBRUARY
RY

FEB FEB
RU RU
ARY ARY

ARY
ARY
RU
FEB
RU

"O Love! how perfect is thy mystic art....
But who, alas! can love, and then be wise?"

—Lord Byron, *Don Juan* (1819)

notes for february

FEBRUARY

2024

SUN	MON	TUE
4	5	6
11	12	13
18	19 Presidents' Day	20
25	26	27

WED	THU	FRI	SAT
	1	2 Groundhog Day Last Quarter Moon ◑	3
7	8	9 New Moon ●	10 Lunar New Year (Year of the Dragon)
14 Valentine's Day Ash Wednesday	15	16 First Quarter Moon ◐	17
21	22	23	24 Full Moon ○
28	29 Leap Day		

FEBRUARY 2024

5 MONDAY

6 TUESDAY

7 WEDNESDAY

8 THURSDAY

9 FRIDAY

New Moon ●

10 SATURDAY

11 SUNDAY

Lunar New Year (Year of the Dragon)

- William S. Burroughs, b. 2/5/1914
- Charles Dickens, b. 2/7/1812
- Laura Ingalls Wilder, b. 2/7/1867
- Sinclair Lewis, b. 2/7/1885
- Gay Talese, b. 2/7/1932
- Jules Verne, b. 2/8/1828
- Kate Chopin, b. 2/8/1851
- Thomas Paine. b. 2/9/1737
- Alice Walker, b. 2/9/1944

FEBRUARY 2024

S	M	T	W	T	F	S
				1	2	3
4	5	6	7	8	9	10
11	12	13	14	15	16	17
18	19	20	21	22	23	24
25	26	27	28	29		

MARCH 2024

S	M	T	W	T	F	S
					1	2
3	4	5	6	7	8	9
10	11	12	13	14	15	16
17	18	19	20	21	22	23
24	25	26	27	28	29	30
31						

12 MONDAY

---

13 TUESDAY

---

14 WEDNESDAY

Valentine's Day
Ash Wednesday

---

15 THURSDAY

16 FRIDAY

First Quarter Moon ◑

17 SATURDAY

18 SUNDAY

NOTES

- Judy Blume, b. 2/12/1938
- Richard Ford, b. 2/16/1944
- Chaim Potok, b. 2/17/1929
- Wallace Stegner, b. 2/18/1909
- Toni Morrison, b. 2/18/1931
- Audre Lorde, b. 2/18/1934

FEBRUARY 2024						
S	M	T	W	T	F	S
				1	2	3
4	5	6	7	8	9	10
11	12	13	14	15	16	17
18	19	20	21	22	23	24
25	26	27	28	29		

MARCH 2024						
S	M	T	W	T	F	S
					1	2
3	4	5	6	7	8	9
10	11	12	13	14	15	16
17	18	19	20	21	22	23
24	25	26	27	28	29	30
31						

FEBRUARY 2024

19 MONDAY

Presidents' Day

20 TUESDAY

21 WEDNESDAY

22 THURSDAY

23 FRIDAY

24 SATURDAY

25 SUNDAY

Full Moon ○

NOTES

- André Breton, b. 2/19/1896
- Carson McCullers, b. 2/19/1917
- Amy Tan, b. 2/19/1952
- Richard Matheson, b. 2/20/1926
- Anaïs Nin, b. 2/21/1903
- W. H. Auden, b. 2/21/1907
- Anthony Burgess, b. 2/25/1917

FEBRUARY 2024

S	M	T	W	T	F	S
				1	2	3
4	5	6	7	8	9	10
11	12	13	14	15	16	17
18	19	20	21	22	23	24
25	26	27	28	29		

MARCH 2024

S	M	T	W	T	F	S
					1	2
3	4	5	6	7	8	9
10	11	12	13	14	15	16
17	18	19	20	21	22	23
24	25	26	27	28	29	30
31						

26 MONDAY

---

27 TUESDAY

---

28 WEDNESDAY

---

29 THURSDAY

Leap Day

1 FRIDAY

---

2 SATURDAY

3 SUNDAY

Last Quarter Moon ◑

NOTES

- Victor Hugo, b. 2/26/1802
- Henry Wadsworth Longfellow, b. 2/27/1807
- Irwin Shaw, b. 2/27/1913
- N. Scott Momaday, b. 2/27/1934
- Ralph Ellison, b. 3/1/1914
- Dr. Seuss, b. 3/2/1904

FEBRUARY 2024

S	M	T	W	T	F	S
				1	2	3
4	5	6	7	8	9	10
11	12	13	14	15	16	17
18	19	20	21	22	23	24
25	26	27	28	29		

MARCH 2024

S	M	T	W	T	F	S
					1	2
3	4	5	6	7	8	9
10	11	12	13	14	15	16
17	18	19	20	21	22	23
24	25	26	27	28	29	30
31						

CAESAR: The ides of March are come.
SOOTHSAYER: Ay, Caesar; but not gone.

—William Shakespeare, *Julius Caesar* (1599)

notes for march

MARCH

2024

SUN	MON	TUE
3 Last Quarter Moon ◐	**4**	**5**
10 Daylight Saving Time Begins (US, CAN) Ramadan (begins at sundown) New Moon ●	**11** Commonwealth Day (UK, CAN, AUS, NZ)	**12**
17 St. Patrick's Day First Quarter Moon ◑	**18**	**19**
24 Palm Sunday Easter **31**	**25** Full Moon ○	**26**

WED	THU	FRI	SAT
		1	2
6	7	8	9
13	14	15	16
20	21	22	23
27	28	29 Good Friday	30

4 MONDAY

5 TUESDAY

6 WEDNESDAY

7 THURSDAY

8 FRIDAY

9 SATURDAY

10 SUNDAY

Daylight Saving Time Begins (US, CAN)
Ramadan (begins at sundown)
New Moon ●

NOTES

- James Ellroy, b. 3/4/1948
- Khaled Hosseini, b. 3/4/1965
- Elizabeth Barrett Browning, b. 3/6/1806
- Gabriel García Márquez, b. 3/6/1927
- Bret Easton Ellis, b. 3/7/1964
- Amanda Gorman, b. 3/7/1998
- Vita Sackville-West, b. 3/9/1892

MARCH 2024

S	M	T	W	T	F	S
					1	2
3	4	5	6	7	8	9
10	11	12	13	14	15	16
17	18	19	20	21	22	23
24	25	26	27	28	29	30
31						

APRIL 2024

S	M	T	W	T	F	S
	1	2	3	4	5	6
7	8	9	10	11	12	13
14	15	16	17	18	19	20
21	22	23	24	25	26	27
28	29	30				

11 MONDAY

Commonwealth Day (UK, CAN, AUS, NZ)

12 TUESDAY

13 WEDNESDAY

14 THURSDAY

15 FRIDAY

16 SATURDAY

17 SUNDAY

St. Patrick's Day
First Quarter Moon ◐

NOTES

- Douglas Adams, b. 3/11/1952
- Dave Eggers, b. 3/12/1970
- Jack Kerouac, b. 3/12/1922
- Hugh Walpole, b. 3/13/1884
- Viet Thanh Nguyen, b. 3/13/1971
- Algernon Blackwood, b. 3/14/1869
- William Gibson, b. 3/17/1948

MARCH 2024

S	M	T	W	T	F	S
					1	2
3	4	5	6	7	8	9
10	11	12	13	14	15	16
17	18	19	20	21	22	23
24	25	26	27	28	29	30
31						

APRIL 2024

S	M	T	W	T	F	S
	1	2	3	4	5	6
7	8	9	10	11	12	13
14	15	16	17	18	19	20
21	22	23	24	25	26	27
28	29	30				

18 MONDAY

---

19 TUESDAY

---

20 WEDNESDAY

---

21 THURSDAY

22 FRIDAY

23 SATURDAY

24 SUNDAY

Palm Sunday

NOTES

- John Updike, b. 3/18/1932
- Philip Roth, b. 3/19/1933
- Henrik Ibsen, b. 3/20/1828
- Lois Lowry, b. 3/20/1937
- Walter Isaacson, b. 3/20/1952
- Louis L'Amour, b. 3/22/1908
- Lawrence Ferlinghetti, b. 3/24/1919

MARCH 2024						
S	M	T	W	T	F	S
					1	2
3	4	5	6	7	8	9
10	11	12	13	14	15	16
17	18	19	20	21	22	23
24	25	26	27	28	29	30
31						

APRIL 2024						
S	M	T	W	T	F	S
	1	2	3	4	5	6
7	8	9	10	11	12	13
14	15	16	17	18	19	20
21	22	23	24	25	26	27
28	29	30				

MARCH 2024

25 MONDAY

Full Moon ○

26 TUESDAY

27 WEDNESDAY

28 THURSDAY

29 FRIDAY

Good Friday

30 SATURDAY

31 SUNDAY

Easter

NOTES

- Flannery O'Connor, b. 3/25/1925
- Gloria Steinem, b. 3/25/1934
- Robert Frost, b. 3/26/1874
- Tennessee Williams, b. 3/26/1911
- Erica Jong, b. 3/26/1942
- Octavio Paz, b. 3/31/1914
- John Fowles, b. 3/31/1926

MARCH 2024

S	M	T	W	T	F	S
					1	2
3	4	5	6	7	8	9
10	11	12	13	14	15	16
17	18	19	20	21	22	23
24	25	26	27	28	29	30
31						

APRIL 2024

S	M	T	W	T	F	S
	1	2	3	4	5	6
7	8	9	10	11	12	13
14	15	16	17	18	19	20
21	22	23	24	25	26	27
28	29	30				

"Of all the months that fill the year
Give April's month to me.
For earth and sky are then so filled
With sweet variety!"

—Letitia Elizabeth Landon, "April" (1823)

notes for april

APRIL

2024

SUN	MON	TUE
	1 Easter Monday (UK) Last Quarter Moon ◐	**2**
7	**8** New Moon ●	**9** Eid al-Fitr (begins at sundown)
14	**15** First Quarter Moon ◑	**16**
21	**22** Earth Day Passover (begins at sundown)	**23** Full Moon ○
28	**29**	**30**

WED	THU	FRI	SAT
3	4	5	6
10	11	12	13
17	18	19	20
24	25 Anzac Day (AUS, NZ)	26	27

1 MONDAY

Easter Monday (UK)
Last Quarter Moon ◐

2 TUESDAY

3 WEDNESDAY

4 THURSDAY

5 FRIDAY

6 SATURDAY

7 SUNDAY

NOTES

- Milan Kundera, b. 4/1/1929
- Hans Christian Andersen, b. 4/2/1805
- Washington Irving, b. 4/3/1783
- Maya Angelou, b. 4/4/1928
- Marguerite Duras, b. 4/4/1914
- Booker T. Washington, b. 4/5/1856

APRIL 2024

S	M	T	W	T	F	S
	1	2	3	4	5	6
7	8	9	10	11	12	13
14	15	16	17	18	19	20
21	22	23	24	25	26	27
28	29	30				

MAY 2024

S	M	T	W	T	F	S
			1	2	3	4
5	6	7	8	9	10	11
12	13	14	15	16	17	18
19	20	21	22	23	24	25
26	27	28	29	30	31	

8 MONDAY

New Moon ●

9 TUESDAY

Eid al-Fitr (begins at sundown)

10 WEDNESDAY

11 THURSDAY

12 FRIDAY

13 SATURDAY

14 SUNDAY

NOTES

- Barbara Kingsolver, b. 4/8/1955
- Paul Theroux, b. 4/10/1941
- Jon Krakauer, b. 4/12/1954
- Samuel Beckett, b. 4/13/1906
- Eudora Welty, b. 4/13/1909

APRIL 2024						
S	M	T	W	T	F	S
	1	2	3	4	5	6
7	8	9	10	11	12	13
14	15	16	17	18	19	20
21	22	23	24	25	26	27
28	29	30				

MAY 2024						
S	M	T	W	T	F	S
			1	2	3	4
5	6	7	8	9	10	11
12	13	14	15	16	17	18
19	20	21	22	23	24	25
26	27	28	29	30	31	

15 MONDAY

First Quarter Moon ◑

16 TUESDAY

17 WEDNESDAY

18 THURSDAY

19 FRIDAY

20 SATURDAY

21 SUNDAY

NOTES

- Henry James, b. 4/15/1843
- John Millington Synge, b. 4/16/1871
- Isak Dinesen, b. 4/17/1885
- Charlotte Brontë, b. 4/21/1816
- Kingsley Amis, b. 4/22/1922

APRIL 2024						
S	M	T	W	T	F	S
	1	2	3	4	5	6
7	8	9	10	11	12	13
14	15	16	17	18	19	20
21	22	23	24	25	26	27
28	29	30				

MAY 2024						
S	M	T	W	T	F	S
			1	2	3	4
5	6	7	8	9	10	11
12	13	14	15	16	17	18
19	20	21	22	23	24	25
26	27	28	29	30	31	

22 MONDAY

Earth Day
Passover (begins at sundown)

23 TUESDAY

Full Moon ○

24 WEDNESDAY

25 THURSDAY

Anzac Day (AUS, NZ)

26 FRIDAY

27 SATURDAY

28 SUNDAY

NOTES

- Henry Fielding, b. 4/22/1707
- Vladimir Nabokov, b. 4/22/1899
- Louise Glück, b. 4/22/1943
- William Shakespeare, bapt. 4/26/1564
- Mary Wollstonecraft, b. 4/27/1759
- Harper Lee, b. 4/28/1926

APRIL 2024						
S	M	T	W	T	F	S
	1	2	3	4	5	6
7	8	9	10	11	12	13
14	15	16	17	18	19	20
21	22	23	24	25	26	27
28	29	30				

MAY 2024						
S	M	T	W	T	F	S
			1	2	3	4
5	6	7	8	9	10	11
12	13	14	15	16	17	18
19	20	21	22	23	24	25
26	27	28	29	30	31	

29 MONDAY

---

30 TUESDAY

---

1 WEDNESDAY

May Day
Last Quarter Moon ◑

---

2 THURSDAY

3 FRIDAY

4 SATURDAY

5 SUNDAY

Orthodox Easter
Cinco de Mayo

NOTES

- Annie Dillard, b. 4/30/1945
- Joseph Heller, b. 5/1/1923
- Niccolò Machiavelli, b. 5/3/1469
- Amos Oz, b. 5/4/1939
- Nellie Bly, b. 5/5/1864

APRIL 2024						
S	M	T	W	T	F	S
	1	2	3	4	5	6
7	8	9	10	11	12	13
14	15	16	17	18	19	20
21	22	23	24	25	26	27
28	29	30				

MAY 2024						
S	M	T	W	T	F	S
			1	2	3	4
5	6	7	8	9	10	11
12	13	14	15	16	17	18
19	20	21	22	23	24	25
26	27	28	29	30	31	

> "One day when the sun had come back over the Forest, bringing with it the scent of May . . . Christopher Robin whistled in a special way he had, and Owl came flying out of the Hundred Acre Wood to see what was wanted."

—A. A. Milne, *Winnie-the-Pooh* (1926)

notes for may

MAY

2024

SUN	MON	TUE
5 Orthodox Easter Cinco de Mayo	**6** May Day bank holiday (UK, IRL)	**7** New Moon ●
12 Mother's Day	**13**	**14**
19	**20** Victoria Day (CAN)	**21**
26	**27** Memorial Day (US) Spring bank holiday (UK)	**28**

WED	THU	FRI	SAT
1 May Day Last Quarter Moon ◗	**2**	**3**	**4**
8	**9**	**10**	**11**
15 First Quarter Moon ◑	**16**	**17**	**18**
22	**23** Full Moon ○	**24**	**25**
29	**30** Last Quarter Moon ◗	**31**	

6 MONDAY

May Day bank holiday (UK, IRL)

7 TUESDAY

New Moon ●

8 WEDNESDAY

9 THURSDAY

10 FRIDAY

11 SATURDAY

12 SUNDAY

Mother's Day

- Robert Browning, b. 5/7/1812
- Rabindranath Tagore, b. 5/7/1861
- Thomas Pynchon, b. 5/8/1937
- Angela Carter, b. 5/7/1940
- J. M. Barrie, b. 5/9/1860
- Dante Gabriel Rossetti, b. 5/12/1828

MAY 2024						
S	M	T	W	T	F	S
			1	2	3	4
5	6	7	8	9	10	11
12	13	14	15	16	17	18
19	20	21	22	23	24	25
26	27	28	29	30	31	

JUNE 2024						
S	M	T	W	T	F	S
						1
2	3	4	5	6	7	8
9	10	11	12	13	14	15
16	17	18	19	20	21	22
23	24	25	26	27	28	29
30						

MAY 2024

13 MONDAY

14 TUESDAY

15 WEDNESDAY

First Quarter Moon ◐

16 THURSDAY

17 FRIDAY

18 SATURDAY

19 SUNDAY

NOTES

- Bruce Chatwin, b. 5/13/1940
- Lorraine Hansberry, b. 5/19/1930
- Daphne du Maurier, b. 5/13/1907
- Armistead Maupin, b. 5/13/1944
- Katherine Anne Porter, b. 5/15/1890
- Jodi Picoult, b. 5/19/1966

MAY 2024						
S	M	T	W	T	F	S
			1	2	3	4
5	6	7	8	9	10	11
12	13	14	15	16	17	18
19	20	21	22	23	24	25
26	27	28	29	30	31	

JUNE 2024						
S	M	T	W	T	F	S
						1
2	3	4	5	6	7	8
9	10	11	12	13	14	15
16	17	18	19	20	21	22
23	24	25	26	27	28	29
30						

20 MONDAY

Victoria Day (CAN)

21 TUESDAY

22 WEDNESDAY

23 THURSDAY

Full Moon ○

24 FRIDAY

25 SATURDAY

26 SUNDAY

NOTES

- Honoré de Balzac, b. 5/20/1799
- Alexander Pope, b. 5/21/1688
- Arthur Conan Doyle, b. 5/22/1859
- Peter Matthiessen, b. 5/22/1927
- Margaret Wise Brown, b. 5/23/1910
- Ralph Waldo Emerson, b. 5/25/1803
- Jamaica Kincaid, b. 5/25/1949

MAY 2024						
S	M	T	W	T	F	S
			1	2	3	4
5	6	7	8	9	10	11
12	13	14	15	16	17	18
19	20	21	22	23	24	25
26	27	28	29	30	31	

JUNE 2024						
S	M	T	W	T	F	S
						1
2	3	4	5	6	7	8
9	10	11	12	13	14	15
16	17	18	19	20	21	22
23	24	25	26	27	28	29
30						

27 MONDAY

Memorial Day (US)
Spring bank holiday (UK)

28 TUESDAY

29 WEDNESDAY

30 THURSDAY

Last Quarter Moon ◑

31 FRIDAY

1 SATURDAY

2 SUNDAY

NOTES

- Dashiell Hammett, b. 5/27/1894
- Rachel Carson, b. 5/27/1907
- John Cheever, b. 5/27/1912
- Herman Wouk, b. 5/27/1915
- T. H. White, b. 5/29/1906
- Walt Whitman, b. 5/31/1819
- Colleen McCullough, b. 6/1/1937
- Thomas Hardy, b. 6/2/1840

MAY 2024

S	M	T	W	T	F	S
			1	2	3	4
5	6	7	8	9	10	11
12	13	14	15	16	17	18
19	20	21	22	23	24	25
26	27	28	29	30	31	

JUNE 2024

S	M	T	W	T	F	S
						1
2	3	4	5	6	7	8
9	10	11	12	13	14	15
16	17	18	19	20	21	22
23	24	25	26	27	28	29
30						

"And so with the sunshine and the great bursts of leaves growing on the trees, just as things grow in fast movies, I had that familiar conviction that life was beginning over again with the summer."

—F. Scott Fitzgerald, *The Great Gatsby* (1925)

notes for june

JUNE

2024

SUN	MON	TUE
2	3	4
9	10	11
16	17	18
Father's Day		
23	24	25
30		

WED	THU	FRI	SAT
			1
5	**6** New Moon ●	**7**	**8**
12	**13**	**14** Flag Day (US) First Quarter Moon ◑	**15**
19 Juneteenth (US)	**20**	**21** Full Moon ○	**22**
26	**27**	**28** Last Quarter Moon ◐	**29**

3 MONDAY

---

4 TUESDAY

---

5 WEDNESDAY

---

6 THURSDAY

New Moon ●

7 FRIDAY

8 SATURDAY

9 SUNDAY

NOTES

- Allen Ginsberg, b. 6/3/1926
- Larry McMurtry, b. 6/3/1936
- Alexander Pushkin, b. 6/6/1799
- Thomas Mann, b. 6/6/1875
- Orhan Pamuk, b. 6/7/1952
- Louise Erdrich, b. 6/7/1954
- Marguerite Yourcenar, b. 6/8/1903

			JUNE 2024			
S	M	T	W	T	F	S
						1
2	3	4	5	6	7	8
9	10	11	12	13	14	15
16	17	18	19	20	21	22
23	24	25	26	27	28	29
30						

			JULY 2024			
S	M	T	W	T	F	S
	1	2	3	4	5	6
7	8	9	10	11	12	13
14	15	16	17	18	19	20
21	22	23	24	25	26	27
28	29	30	31			

10 MONDAY

---

11 TUESDAY

---

12 WEDNESDAY

---

13 THURSDAY

14 FRIDAY

Flag Day (US)
First Quarter Moon ☽

15 SATURDAY

16 SUNDAY

Father's Day

NOTES

- Saul Bellow, b. 6/10/1915
- William Styron, b. 6/11/1925
- Anne Frank, b. 6/12/1929
- Johanna Spyri, b. 6/12/1827
- Dorothy Sayers, b. 6/13/1893
- Harriet Beecher Stowe, b. 6/14/1811
- Joyce Carol Oates, b. 6/16/1938

JUNE 2024						
S	M	T	W	T	F	S
						1
2	3	4	5	6	7	8
9	10	11	12	13	14	15
16	17	18	19	20	21	22
23	24	25	26	27	28	29
30						

JULY 2024						
S	M	T	W	T	F	S
	1	2	3	4	5	6
7	8	9	10	11	12	13
14	15	16	17	18	19	20
21	22	23	24	25	26	27
28	29	30	31			

JUNE 2024

17 MONDAY

---

18 TUESDAY

---

19 WEDNESDAY

Juneteenth (US)

---

20 THURSDAY

21 FRIDAY

Full Moon ○

22 SATURDAY

23 SUNDAY

NOTES

- Salman Rushdie, b. 6/19/1947
- Mary McCarthy, b. 6/21/1912
- Richard Powers, b. 6/18/1957
- Jean-Paul Sartre, b. 6/21/1905
- Ian McEwan, b. 6/21/1948
- Erich Maria Remarque, b. 6/22/1898

		JUNE 2024				
S	M	T	W	T	F	S
						1
2	3	4	5	6	7	8
9	10	11	12	13	14	15
16	17	18	19	20	21	22
23	24	25	26	27	28	29
30						

		JULY 2024				
S	M	T	W	T	F	S
	1	2	3	4	5	6
7	8	9	10	11	12	13
14	15	16	17	18	19	20
21	22	23	24	25	26	27
28	29	30	31			

24 MONDAY

---

25 TUESDAY

---

26 WEDNESDAY

---

27 THURSDAY

28 FRIDAY

Last Quarter Moon ◗

29 SATURDAY

30 SUNDAY

NOTES

- George Orwell, b. 6/25/1903
- Pearl S. Buck, b. 6/26/1892
- Paul Laurence Dunbar, b. 6/27/1872
- E. R. Braithwaite, b. 6/27/1912
- Jean-Jacques Rousseau, b. 6/28/1712
- Antoine de Saint-Exupéry, b. 6/29/1900

		JUNE 2024				
S	M	T	W	T	F	S
						1
2	3	4	5	6	7	8
9	10	11	12	13	14	15
16	17	18	19	20	21	22
23	24	25	26	27	28	29
30						

		JULY 2024				
S	M	T	W	T	F	S
	1	2	3	4	5	6
7	8	9	10	11	12	13
14	15	16	17	18	19	20
21	22	23	24	25	26	27
28	29	30	31			

july

JULY

JULY JULY

july

july

july

july

> **"It was a hot, hot day near the end of July. . . .
> Even conversation had collapsed under the heat."**
>
> —Zora Neale Thurston, "Sweat" (1926)

notes for july

SUN	MON	TUE
	1 Canada Day	**2**
7	**8**	**9**
14	**15**	**16**
21 Full Moon ○	**22**	**23**
28	**29**	**30**

JULY

2024

WED	THU	FRI	SAT
3	4 Independence Day (US)	5 New Moon ●	6
10	11	12	13 First Quarter Moon ◗
17	18	19	20
24	25	26	27 Last Quarter Moon ◖
31			

JULY 2024

1 MONDAY

Canada Day

2 TUESDAY

3 WEDNESDAY

4 THURSDAY

Independence Day (US)

5 FRIDAY

New Moon ●

6 SATURDAY

7 SUNDAY

NOTES

- George Sand, b. 7/1/1804
- Susan Glaspell, b. 7/1/1876
- Hermann Hesse, b. 7/2/1877
- Franz Kafka, b. 7/3/1883
- Nathaniel Hawthorne, b. 7/4/1804
- Jean Cocteau, b. 7/5/1889

JULY 2024						
S	M	T	W	T	F	S
	1	2	3	4	5	6
7	8	9	10	11	12	13
14	15	16	17	18	19	20
21	22	23	24	25	26	27
28	29	30	31			

AUGUST 2024						
S	M	T	W	T	F	S
				1	2	3
4	5	6	7	8	9	10
11	12	13	14	15	16	17
18	19	20	21	22	23	24
25	26	27	28	29	30	31

8 MONDAY

9 TUESDAY

10 WEDNESDAY

11 THURSDAY

12 FRIDAY

13 SATURDAY

14 SUNDAY

First Quarter Moon ◐

NOTES

- Mervyn Peake, b. 7/9/1911
- Marcel Proust, b. 7/10/1871
- E. B. White, b. 7/11/1899
- Jhumpa Lahiri, b. 7/11/1967
- Henry David Thoreau, b. 7/12/1817
- Pablo Neruda, b. 7/12/1904
- Irving Stone, b. 7/14/1903

			JULY 2024			
S	M	T	W	T	F	S
	1	2	3	4	5	6
7	8	9	10	11	12	13
14	15	16	17	18	19	20
21	22	23	24	25	26	27
28	29	30	31			

			AUGUST 2024			
S	M	T	W	T	F	S
				1	2	3
4	5	6	7	8	9	10
11	12	13	14	15	16	17
18	19	20	21	22	23	24
25	26	27	28	29	30	31

15 MONDAY

16 TUESDAY

17 WEDNESDAY

18 THURSDAY

19 FRIDAY

20 SATURDAY

21 SUNDAY

Full Moon ○

NOTES

- Iris Murdoch, b. 7/15/1919
- Richard Russo, b. 7/15/1949
- Anita Brookner, b. 7/16/1928
- Hunter S. Thompson, b. 7/18/1937
- Cormac McCarthy, b. 7/20/1933
- Alistair MacLeod, b. 7/20/1936
- Ernest Hemingway, b. 7/21/1899

JULY 2024						
S	M	T	W	T	F	S
	1	2	3	4	5	6
7	8	9	10	11	12	13
14	15	16	17	18	19	20
21	22	23	24	25	26	27
28	29	30	31			

AUGUST 2024						
S	M	T	W	T	F	S
				1	2	3
4	5	6	7	8	9	10
11	12	13	14	15	16	17
18	19	20	21	22	23	24
25	26	27	28	29	30	31

22 MONDAY

---

23 TUESDAY

---

24 WEDNESDAY

---

25 THURSDAY

26 FRIDAY

27 SATURDAY

28 SUNDAY

Last Quarter Moon ◗

NOTES

- Emma Lazarus, b. 7/22/1849
- Raymond Chandler, b. 7/23/1888
- Alexandre Dumas, b. 7/24/1802
- George Bernard Shaw, b. 7/26/1856
- Aldous Huxley, b. 7/26/1894
- Beatrix Potter, b. 7/28/1866
- John Ashbery, b. 7/28/1927

JULY 2024						
S	M	T	W	T	F	S
	1	2	3	4	5	6
7	8	9	10	11	12	13
14	15	16	17	18	19	20
21	22	23	24	25	26	27
28	29	30	31			

AUGUST 2024						
S	M	T	W	T	F	S
				1	2	3
4	5	6	7	8	9	10
11	12	13	14	15	16	17
18	19	20	21	22	23	24
25	26	27	28	29	30	31

29 MONDAY

30 TUESDAY

31 WEDNESDAY

1 THURSDAY

2 FRIDAY

3 SATURDAY

4 SUNDAY

New Moon ●

NOTES

- Chester Himes, b. 7/29/1909
- Emily Brontë, b. 7/30/1818
- Primo Levi, b. 7/31/1919
- Herman Melville, b. 8/1/1819
- James Baldwin, b. 8/2/1924
- Isabel Allende, b. 8/2/1942
- P. D. James, b. 8/3/1920
- Percy Bysshe Shelley, b. 8/4/1792

JULY 2024						
S	M	T	W	T	F	S
	1	2	3	4	5	6
7	8	9	10	11	12	13
14	15	16	17	18	19	20
21	22	23	24	25	26	27
28	29	30	31			

AUGUST 2024						
S	M	T	W	T	F	S
				1	2	3
4	5	6	7	8	9	10
11	12	13	14	15	16	17
18	19	20	21	22	23	24
25	26	27	28	29	30	31

AUGUST

augus
augus
augus

AUG
UST

AUG
UST
AUGUST

> "Sirius rises late in the dark, liquid sky
> On summer nights, star of stars,
> Orion's Dog they call it, brightest
> Of all."

—Homer, *The Iliad* (c. 8th century BCE)

notes for august

AUGUST

SUN	MON	TUE
4 New Moon ●	**5**	**6**
11	**12** First Quarter Moon ◑	**13**
18	**19** Full Moon ○	**20**
25	**26** Summer Bank Holiday (UK) Last Quarter Moon ◑	**27**

2024

WED	THU	FRI	SAT
	1	2	3
7	8	9	10
14	15	16	17
21	22	23	24
28	29	30	31

AUGUST 2024

5 MONDAY

6 TUESDAY

7 WEDNESDAY

8 THURSDAY

9 FRIDAY

10 SATURDAY

11 SUNDAY

- Guy de Maupassant, b. 8/5/1850
- Sara Teasdale, b. 8/8/1884
- Daniel Keyes, b. 8/9/1927
- Jorge Amado, b. 8/10/1912
- Suzanne Collins, b. 8/10/1962
- Alex Haley, b. 8/11/1921

AUGUST 2024

S	M	T	W	T	F	S
				1	2	3
4	5	6	7	8	9	10
11	12	13	14	15	16	17
18	19	20	21	22	23	24
25	26	27	28	29	30	31

SEPTEMBER 2024

S	M	T	W	T	F	S
1	2	3	4	5	6	7
8	9	10	11	12	13	14
15	16	17	18	19	20	21
22	23	24	25	26	27	28
29	30					

AUGUST 2024

12 MONDAY

First Quarter Moon ◗

13 TUESDAY

14 WEDNESDAY

15 THURSDAY

16 FRIDAY

---

17 SATURDAY

18 SUNDAY

NOTES

- William Goldman, b. 8/12/1931
- Letitia Elizabeth Landon, b. 8/14/1802
- Edna Ferber, b. 8/15/1885
- Charles Bukowski, 8/16/1920
- V. S. Naipaul, b. 8/17/1932

AUGUST 2024

S	M	T	W	T	F	S
				1	2	3
4	5	6	7	8	9	10
11	12	13	14	15	16	17
18	19	20	21	22	23	24
25	26	27	28	29	30	31

SEPTEMBER 2024

S	M	T	W	T	F	S
1	2	3	4	5	6	7
8	9	10	11	12	13	14
15	16	17	18	19	20	21
22	23	24	25	26	27	28
29	30					

AUGUST 2024

19 MONDAY

Full Moon ○

20 TUESDAY

21 WEDNESDAY

22 THURSDAY

23 FRIDAY

24 SATURDAY

25 SUNDAY

NOTES

- Ogden Nash, b. 8/19/1902
- Frank McCourt, b. 8/19/1930
- H. P. Lovecraft, 8/20/1890
- Ray Bradbury, b. 8/22/1920
- Annie Proulx, b. 8/22/1935
- Dorothy Parker, b. 8/22/1893
- Jorge Luis Borges, b. 8/24/1899
- A. S. Byatt b. 8/24/1936
- Martin Amis, b. 8/25/1949

AUGUST 2024						
S	M	T	W	T	F	S
				1	2	3
4	5	6	7	8	9	10
11	12	13	14	15	16	17
18	19	20	21	22	23	24
25	26	27	28	29	30	31

SEPTEMBER 2024						
S	M	T	W	T	F	S
1	2	3	4	5	6	7
8	9	10	11	12	13	14
15	16	17	18	19	20	21
22	23	24	25	26	27	28
29	30					

26 MONDAY

Summer Bank Holiday (UK)
Last Quarter Moon ◗

27 TUESDAY

28 WEDNESDAY

29 THURSDAY

30 FRIDAY

31 SATURDAY

1 SUNDAY

NOTES

- Theodore Dreiser, b. 8/27/1871
- Johann Wolfgang von Goethe
  b. 8/28/1749
- Rita Dove, b. 8/28/1952
- Oliver Wendell Holmes Sr.,
  b. 8/29/1809
- Mary Shelley, b. 8/30/1797
- Edgar Rice Burroughs, b. 9/1/1875

AUGUST 2024						
S	M	T	W	T	F	S
				1	2	3
4	5	6	7	8	9	10
11	12	13	14	15	16	17
18	19	20	21	22	23	24
25	26	27	28	29	30	31

SEPTEMBER 2024						
S	M	T	W	T	F	S
1	2	3	4	5	6	7
8	9	10	11	12	13	14
15	16	17	18	19	20	21
22	23	24	25	26	27	28
29	30					

SEPTEMBER

SEP
TEM
BER

Sep

"Her pleasure in the walk must arise from . . . repeating to herself some few of the thousand poetical descriptions extant of autumn."

—Jane Austen, *Persuasion* (1818)

notes for september

SEPTEMBER

2024

SUN	MON	TUE
1	2 Labor Day (US, CAN) New Moon ●	3
8	9	10
15	16	17 Full Moon ○
22	23	24 Last Quarter Moon ◑
29	30	

WED	THU	FRI	SAT
4	5	6	7
11 First Quarter Moon ◑	12	13	14
18	19	20	21
25	26	27	28

2 MONDAY

Labor Day (US, CAN)
New Moon ●

3 TUESDAY

4 WEDNESDAY

5 THURSDAY

6 FRIDAY

7 SATURDAY

8 SUNDAY

NOTES

- Richard Wright, b. 9/4/1908
- Robert M. Pirsig, 9/6/1928
- Jennifer Egan, b. 9/7/1962
- Siegfried Sassoon, b. 9/8/1886
- Ann Beattie, b. 9/8/1947

SEPTEMBER 2024						
S	M	T	W	T	F	S
1	2	3	4	5	6	7
8	9	10	11	12	13	14
15	16	17	18	19	20	21
22	23	24	25	26	27	28
29	30					

OCTOBER 2024						
S	M	T	W	T	F	S
		1	2	3	4	5
6	7	8	9	10	11	12
13	14	15	16	17	18	19
20	21	22	23	24	25	26
27	28	29	30	31		

9 MONDAY

---

10 TUESDAY

---

11 WEDNESDAY

First Quarter Moon ◗

---

12 THURSDAY

13 FRIDAY

14 SATURDAY

15 SUNDAY

NOTES

- Leo Tolstoy, b. 9/9/1828
- Jared Diamond, b. 9/10/1937
- O. Henry, b. 9/11/1862
- D. H. Lawrence, b. 9/11/1885
- Michael Ondaatje, b. 9/12/1943
- Roald Dahl, b. 9/13/1916
- James Fenimore Cooper, b. 9/15/1789
- Agatha Christie, b. 9/15/1890

SEPTEMBER 2024						
S	M	T	W	T	F	S
1	2	3	4	5	6	7
8	9	10	11	12	13	14
15	16	17	18	19	20	21
22	23	24	25	26	27	28
29	30					

OCTOBER 2024						
S	M	T	W	T	F	S
		1	2	3	4	5
6	7	8	9	10	11	12
13	14	15	16	17	18	19
20	21	22	23	24	25	26
27	28	29	30	31		

16 MONDAY

---

17 TUESDAY

Full Moon ○

---

18 WEDNESDAY

---

19 THURSDAY

20 FRIDAY

21 SATURDAY

22 SUNDAY

NOTES

- Ken Kesey, b. 9/17/1935
- Samuel Johnson, b. 9/18/1709
- William Golding, b. 9/19/1911
- Upton Sinclair, b. 9/20/1878
- George R. R. Martin, b. 9/20/1948
- H. G. Wells, 9/21/1866
- Stephen King, b. 9/21/1947
- Rosamunde Pilcher, b. 9/22/1924

SEPTEMBER 2024

S	M	T	W	T	F	S
1	2	3	4	5	6	7
8	9	10	11	12	13	14
15	16	17	18	19	20	21
22	23	24	25	26	27	28
29	30					

OCTOBER 2024

S	M	T	W	T	F	S
		1	2	3	4	5
6	7	8	9	10	11	12
13	14	15	16	17	18	19
20	21	22	23	24	25	26
27	28	29	30	31		

23 MONDAY

---

24 TUESDAY

Last Quarter Moon ◑

---

25 WEDNESDAY

---

26 THURSDAY

27 FRIDAY

28 SATURDAY

29 SUNDAY

NOTES

- F. Scott Fitzgerald, b. 9/24/1896
- William Faulkner, b. 9/25/1897
- bell hooks, b. 9/25/1952
- T. S. Eliot, b. 9/26/1888
- Miguel de Cervantes, b. 9/29/1547

SEPTEMBER 2024						
S	M	T	W	T	F	S
1	2	3	4	5	6	7
8	9	10	11	12	13	14
15	16	17	18	19	20	21
22	23	24	25	26	27	28
29	30					

OCTOBER 2024						
S	M	T	W	T	F	S
		1	2	3	4	5
6	7	8	9	10	11	12
13	14	15	16	17	18	19
20	21	22	23	24	25	26
27	28	29	30	31		

30 MONDAY

---

1 TUESDAY

---

2 WEDNESDAY

Rosh Hashanah (begins at sundown)
New Moon ●

---

3 THURSDAY

4 FRIDAY

5 SATURDAY

6 SUNDAY

NOTES

- Truman Capote, b. 9/30/1924
- Elie Wiesel, b. 9/30/1928
- Laura Esquivel, b. 9/30/1950
- Ta-Nehisi Coates, b. 9/30/1975
- Graham Greene, b. 10/2/1904
- Gore Vidal, b. 10/3/1925
- Jackie Collins, b. 10/4/1937
- Anne Rice, b. 10/4/1941
- Václav Havel, b. 10/5/1936

SEPTEMBER 2024

S	M	T	W	T	F	S
	1	2	3	4	5	6	7
8	9	10	11	12	13	14
15	16	17	18	19	20	21
22	23	24	25	26	27	28
29	30					

OCTOBER 2024

S	M	T	W	T	F	S
		1	2	3	4	5
6	7	8	9	10	11	12
13	14	15	16	17	18	19
20	21	22	23	24	25	26
27	28	29	30	31		

OC
TO
BER

OCTOB

"During the whole of a dull, dark, and soundless day in the autumn . . . [I] found myself, as the shades of the evening drew on, within view of the melancholy House of Usher."

—Edgar Allan Poe, "The Fall of the House of Usher" (1839)

notes for october

OCTOBER

2024

SUN	MON	TUE
		1
6	7	8
13	14	15
	Indigenous Peoples' Day Columbus Day (US) Thanksgiving (CAN)	
20	21	22
27	28	29

WED	THU	FRI	SAT
2 Rosh Hashanah (begins at sundown) New Moon ●	**3**	**4**	**5**
9	**10** First Quarter Moon ◗	**11** Yom Kippur (begins at sundown)	**12**
16	**17** Full Moon ○	**18**	**19**
23	**24** Last Quarter Moon ◗	**25**	**26**
30	**31** Halloween		

7 MONDAY

8 TUESDAY

9 WEDNESDAY

10 THURSDAY

First Quarter Moon ◑

11 FRIDAY

Yom Kippur (begins at sundown)

12 SATURDAY

13 SUNDAY

NOTES

- Thomas Keneally, b. 10/7/1935
- Frank Herbert, b. 10/8/1920
- James Clavell, b. 10/10/1921
- Elmore Leonard, b. 10/11/1925
- Richard Price, b. 10/12/1949

OCTOBER 2024

S	M	T	W	T	F	S
		1	2	3	4	5
6	7	8	9	10	11	12
13	14	15	16	17	18	19
20	21	22	23	24	25	26
27	28	29	30	31		

NOVEMBER 2024

S	M	T	W	T	F	S
					1	2
3	4	5	6	7	8	9
10	11	12	13	14	15	16
17	18	19	20	21	22	23
24	25	26	27	28	29	30

14 MONDAY

Indigenous Peoples' Day
Columbus Day (US)
Thanksgiving (CAN)

15 TUESDAY

16 WEDNESDAY

17 THURSDAY

Full Moon ○

18 FRIDAY

---

19 SATURDAY | **20 SUNDAY**

NOTES

- e. e. cummings, b. 10/14/1894
- P. G. Wodehouse, b. 10/15/1881
- Ntozake Shange, b. 10/18/1948
- Oscar Wilde, b. 10/16/1854
- Günter Grass, b. 10/16/1927
- Arthur Miller b. 10/17/1915
- Terry McMillan, b. 10/18/1951
- John le Carré, b. 10/19/1931

OCTOBER 2024

S	M	T	W	T	F	S
		1	2	3	4	5
6	7	8	9	10	11	12
13	14	15	16	17	18	19
20	21	22	23	24	25	26
27	28	29	30	31		

NOVEMBER 2024

S	M	T	W	T	F	S
					1	2
3	4	5	6	7	8	9
10	11	12	13	14	15	16
17	18	19	20	21	22	23
24	25	26	27	28	29	30

21 MONDAY

22 TUESDAY

23 WEDNESDAY

24 THURSDAY

Last Quarter Moon ◑

25 FRIDAY

26 SATURDAY

27 SUNDAY

NOTES

- Samuel Taylor Coleridge, b. 10/21/1772
- Ursula K. Le Guin, b. 10/21/1929
- Doris Lessing, b. 10/22/1919
- Michael Crichton, b. 10/23/1942
- Denise Levertov, b. 10/24/1923
- Anne Tyler, b. 10/25/1941
- Zadie Smith, b. 10/25/1975
- Dylan Thomas, b. 10/27/1914
- Sylvia Plath, b. 10/27/1932

OCTOBER 2024

S	M	T	W	T	F	S
		1	2	3	4	5
6	7	8	9	10	11	12
13	14	15	16	17	18	19
20	21	22	23	24	25	26
27	28	29	30	31		

NOVEMBER 2024

S	M	T	W	T	F	S
					1	2
3	4	5	6	7	8	9
10	11	12	13	14	15	16
17	18	19	20	21	22	23
24	25	26	27	28	29	30

28 MONDAY

---

29 TUESDAY

---

30 WEDNESDAY

---

31 THURSDAY

Halloween

1 FRIDAY

New Moon ●

2 SATURDAY

3 SUNDAY

Daylight Saving Time Ends (US, CAN)

NOTES

- Robert Caro, b. 10/30/1935
- John Keats, b. 10/31/1795
- Stephen Crane, b. 11/1/1871
- Susanna Clarke, b. 11/1/1959
- William Cullen Bryant, b. 11/3/1794

OCTOBER 2024						
S	M	T	W	T	F	S
		1	2	3	4	5
6	7	8	9	10	11	12
13	14	15	16	17	18	19
20	21	22	23	24	25	26
27	28	29	30	31		

NOVEMBER 2024						
S	M	T	W	T	F	S
					1	2
3	4	5	6	7	8	9
10	11	12	13	14	15	16
17	18	19	20	21	22	23
24	25	26	27	28	29	30

NOVEMBER

NOVEMBER

november

notes for november

NOVEMBER

2024

SUN	MON	TUE
3 Daylight Saving Time Ends (US, CAN)	4	5 Election Day (US)
10	11 Veterans Day (US)	12
17	18	19
24	25	26

WED	THU	FRI	SAT
		1 New Moon ●	2
6	7	8	9 First Quarter Moon ◗
13	14	15 Full Moon ○	16
20	21	22 Last Quarter Moon ◑	23
27	28 Thanksgiving (US)	29	30

NOVEMBER 2024

4 MONDAY

5 TUESDAY

Election Day (US)

6 WEDNESDAY

7 THURSDAY

8 FRIDAY

9 SATURDAY

10 SUNDAY

First Quarter Moon ◑

NOTES

- Ida Tarbell, b. 11/5/1857
- Colson Whitehead, b. 11/6/1969
- Albert Camus, b. 11/7/1913
- Bram Stoker, b. 11/8/1847
- Margaret Mitchell, b. 11/8/1900
- Kazuo Ishiguro, b. 11/8/1954
- Neil Gaiman, b. 11/10/1960

NOVEMBER 2024						
S	M	T	W	T	F	S
					1	2
3	4	5	6	7	8	9
10	11	12	13	14	15	16
17	18	19	20	21	22	23
24	25	26	27	28	29	30

DECEMBER 2024						
S	M	T	W	T	F	S
1	2	3	4	5	6	7
8	9	10	11	12	13	14
15	16	17	18	19	20	21
22	23	24	25	26	27	28
29	30	31				

11 MONDAY

Veterans Day (US)

12 TUESDAY

13 WEDNESDAY

14 THURSDAY

15 FRIDAY

Full Moon ○

16 SATURDAY

17 SUNDAY

NOTES

- Fyodor Dostoevsky, b. 11/11/1821
- Carlos Fuentes, b. 11/11/1928
- Kurt Vonnegut, b. 11/11/1922
- Robert Louis Stevenson, b. 11/13/1850
- Astrid Lindgren, b. 11/14/1907
- J. G. Ballard, b. 11/15/1930
- Liane Moriarty, b. 11/15/1966
- Chinua Achebe, b. 11/16/1930

NOVEMBER 2024

S	M	T	W	T	F	S
					1	2
3	4	5	6	7	8	9
10	11	12	13	14	15	16
17	18	19	20	21	22	23
24	25	26	27	28	29	30

DECEMBER 2024

S	M	T	W	T	F	S
1	2	3	4	5	6	7
8	9	10	11	12	13	14
15	16	17	18	19	20	21
22	23	24	25	26	27	28
29	30	31				

18 MONDAY

19 TUESDAY

20 WEDNESDAY

21 THURSDAY

22 FRIDAY

Last Quarter Moon ◑

23 SATURDAY

24 SUNDAY

NOTES

- Margaret Atwood, b. 11/18/1939
- Nadine Gordimer, b. 11/20/1923
- Don DeLillo, b. 11/20/1936
- Isaac Bashevis Singer, b. 11/21/1902
- George Eliot, b. 11/22/1819
- André Gide, b. 11/22/1869
- Frances Hodgson Burnett, b. 11/24/1849
- Arundhati Roy, b. 11/24/1961

NOVEMBER 2024						
S	M	T	W	T	F	S
					1	2
3	4	5	6	7	8	9
10	11	12	13	14	15	16
17	18	19	20	21	22	23
24	25	26	27	28	29	30

DECEMBER 2024						
S	M	T	W	T	F	S
1	2	3	4	5	6	7
8	9	10	11	12	13	14
15	16	17	18	19	20	21
22	23	24	25	26	27	28
29	30	31				

25 MONDAY

26 TUESDAY

27 WEDNESDAY

28 THURSDAY

Thanksgiving (US)

29 FRIDAY

30 SATURDAY

1 SUNDAY

New Moon ●

NOTES

- Eugène Ionesco, b. 11/26/1909
- James Agee, b. 11/27/1909
- Louisa May Alcott, b. 11/29/1832
- C. S. Lewis, b. 11/29/1898
- Madeleine L'Engle, b. 11/29/1918
- Mark Twain, b. 11/30/1835
- L. M. Montgomery, b. 11/30/1874
- Candace Bushnell, b. 12/1/1958

NOVEMBER 2024

S	M	T	W	T	F	S
					1	2
3	4	5	6	7	8	9
10	11	12	13	14	15	16
17	18	19	20	21	22	23
24	25	26	27	28	29	30

DECEMBER 2024

S	M	T	W	T	F	S
1	2	3	4	5	6	7
8	9	10	11	12	13	14
15	16	17	18	19	20	21
22	23	24	25	26	27	28
29	30	31				

DECEMBER

DECEMBER

december

DECEMBER

DECEMBER

"From other branches hung gilded apples and walnuts, as if they had grown there; and above, and all round, were hundreds of red, blue, and white tapers . . . and at the very top was fastened a glittering star, made of tinsel. Oh, it was very beautiful!"

—Hans Christian Andersen, "The Fir Tree" (1844)

notes for december

DECEMBER

2024

SUN	MON	TUE
1 New Moon ●	**2**	**3**
8 First Quarter Moon ◑	**9**	**10**
15 Full Moon ○	**16**	**17**
22 Last Quarter Moon ◐	**23**	**24**
29	**30** New Moon ●	**31** New Year's Eve

WED	THU	FRI	SAT
4	5	6	7
11	12	13	14
18	19	20	21
25 Christmas Day Hanukkah (begins at sundown)	26 Kwanzaa Boxing Day (CAN, UK)	27	28

2 MONDAY

---

3 TUESDAY

---

4 WEDNESDAY

---

5 THURSDAY

6 FRIDAY

7 SATURDAY

8 SUNDAY

First Quarter Moon ◗

NOTES

- T. C. Boyle, b. 12/2/1948
- Ann Patchett, b. 12/2/1963
- Rainier Maria Rilke, b. 12/4/1875
- Joan Didion, b. 12/5/1934
- Calvin Trillin, b. 12/5/1935
- Willa Cather, b. 12/7/1873
- James Thurber, b. 12/8/1894

DECEMBER 2024

S	M	T	W	T	F	S
1	2	3	4	5	6	7
8	9	10	11	12	13	14
15	16	17	18	19	20	21
22	23	24	25	26	27	28
29	30	31				

JANUARY 2025

S	M	T	W	T	F	S
			1	2	3	4
5	6	7	8	9	10	11
12	13	14	15	16	17	18
19	20	21	22	23	24	25
26	27	28	29	30	31	

DECEMBER 2024

9 MONDAY

10 TUESDAY

11 WEDNESDAY

12 THURSDAY

13 FRIDAY

14 SATURDAY

15 SUNDAY

Full Moon ○

NOTES

- John Milton, b. 12/9/1608
- Emily Dickinson, b. 12/10/1830
- Naguib Mahfouz, b. 12/11/1911
- Aleksandr Solzhenitsyn, b. 12/11/1918
- Colleen Hoover, b. 12/11/1979
- Gustave Flaubert, b. 12/12/1821
- Shirley Jackson, b. 12/14/1916
- Edna O'Brien, b. 12/15/1930

DECEMBER 2024

S	M	T	W	T	F	S
	1	2	3	4	5	6	7
8	9	10	11	12	13	14
15	16	17	18	19	20	21
22	23	24	25	26	27	28
29	30	31				

JANUARY 2025

S	M	T	W	T	F	S
			1	2	3	4
5	6	7	8	9	10	11
12	13	14	15	16	17	18
19	20	21	22	23	24	25
26	27	28	29	30	31	

DECEMBER 2024

16 MONDAY

17 TUESDAY

18 WEDNESDAY

19 THURSDAY

20 FRIDAY

21 SATURDAY

22 SUNDAY

Last Quarter Moon ◐

NOTES

- Jane Austen, b. 12/16/1775
- H. H. Munro (Saki), b. 12/18/1870
- Kate Atkinson, b. 12/20/1951
- Sandra Cisneros, b. 12/20/1954
- Rebecca West, b. 12/21/1892

DECEMBER 2024

S	M	T	W	T	F	S
1	2	3	4	5	6	7
8	9	10	11	12	13	14
15	16	17	18	19	20	21
22	23	24	25	26	27	28
29	30	31				

JANUARY 2025

S	M	T	W	T	F	S
			1	2	3	4
5	6	7	8	9	10	11
12	13	14	15	16	17	18
19	20	21	22	23	24	25
26	27	28	29	30	31	

23 MONDAY

---

24 TUESDAY

---

25 WEDNESDAY

Christmas Day
Hanukkah (begins at sundown)

---

26 THURSDAY

Kwanzaa
Boxing Day (CAN, UK)

27 FRIDAY

28 SATURDAY

29 SUNDAY

NOTES

- Donna Tartt, b. 12/23/1963
- Mary Higgins Clark, b. 12/24/1927
- Carlos Castañeda, b. 12/25/1925
- Henry Miller, b. 12/26/1891
- David Sedaris, b. 12/26/1956
- Stan Lee, b. 12/28/1922
- William Gaddis, b. 12/29/1922

DECEMBER 2024

S	M	T	W	T	F	S
1	2	3	4	5	6	7
8	9	10	11	12	13	14
15	16	17	18	19	20	21
22	23	24	25	26	27	28
29	30	31				

JANUARY 2025

S	M	T	W	T	F	S
			1	2	3	4
5	6	7	8	9	10	11
12	13	14	15	16	17	18
19	20	21	22	23	24	25
26	27	28	29	30	31	

DEC 2024 / JAN 2025

30 MONDAY

New Moon ●

31 TUESDAY

New Year's Eve

1 WEDNESDAY

New Year's Day

2 THURSDAY

3 FRIDAY

4 SATURDAY

5 SUNDAY

NOTES

- Paul Bowles, b. 12/30/1910
- Junot Díaz, b. 12/31/1968
- E. M. Forster, b. 1/1/1879
- J. D. Salinger, b. 1/1/1919
- Isaac Asimov, b. c. 1/2/1920
- J. R. R. Tolkien, b. 1/3/1892
- Erik Larson, b. 1/3/1954
- Umberto Eco, b. 1/5/1932

DECEMBER 2024

S	M	T	W	T	F	S
1	2	3	4	5	6	7
8	9	10	11	12	13	14
15	16	17	18	19	20	21
22	23	24	25	26	27	28
29	30	31				

JANUARY 2025

S	M	T	W	T	F	S
			1	2	3	4
5	6	7	8	9	10	11
12	13	14	15	16	17	18
19	20	21	22	23	24	25
26	27	28	29	30	31	

NOTES

NOTES

UNION SQUARE & CO.

NEW YORK

ISBN 978-1-4549-4961-9

For information about custom editions,
special sales, and premium purchases, please contact
specialsales@unionsquareandco.com.

Printed in China

2 4 6 8 10 9 7 5 3 1

unionsquareandco.com

Text compiled by Barbara M. Berger
Cover design by Christine Heun and Jo Obarowski
Interior design by Christine Heun